Why Do Birds Fly?

How to Fly High in a World trying to Keep you Down

DR. ARNOLD O. THOMPSON

Photos and Illustrations By Author

Printed in the United States of America

ISBN 979-8-89114-012-7 (sc)
ISBN 979-8-89114-014-1 (hc)
ISBN 979-8-89114-013-4 (e)

Library of Congress Control Number: 2023918171

2023.09.29

MainSpring Books
5901 W. Century Blvd
Suite 750
Los Angeles, CA, US, 90045

www.mainspringbooks.com

Contents

Introduction: Our Wild World of Birds v

1 "Wings" 1

2 "Will" 8

3 "Way" 14

4 Work 26

5 "Wonder" 32

6 "Worry" 39

7 "World" 42

8 Wisdom 45

9 Winning Dreams – Words to be Wise 51

Photos of Inspiration and personality 55

In-House Book Review 71

Introduction:
Our Wild World of Birds

Like hearts filled with joy songbirds share their melodious tunes as they pause, fly, and play together in the open spaces of our world. They fly with the serious purpose of playing and parading their inner joy.

I love birds. I have had the privilege of photographing some of the world-famous and powerful people. And I feel honored to have done that. But I must admit there is an extra delight for me just photographing birds. It is like professionally coming home to the nature of things: A love of the earth and the world, yet with a strong desire to fly above them all. I often took my camera out quickly to take a picture and within a wink, a brief pause, they take to the skies mounting, turning, and flipping like being possessed with a basic joy just to be alive; just to fly. This inherent joy of life among birds we cannot let it fade among us. We pursue activities to find joy. Birds act to show they already found it.

This is the basic lesson of birds to us humans. Happiness is something futile to pursue if you do not already have it. Life like that of the birds, they show what they already have in their little hearts. We too can develop what the birds have this wonderful happy heart. It takes a happy heart to fly above everything else. There are no sadness in the sky. So, discover the joy of flying with the birds.

As I study the actions of birds; their frolicking and dancing, listening to the flaps of their wings, and the language of their tweets, how would they respond the question "How are you?" I think I hear them tweet "We are just happy to be alive." They make me feel that way when I photograph them in abundance together.

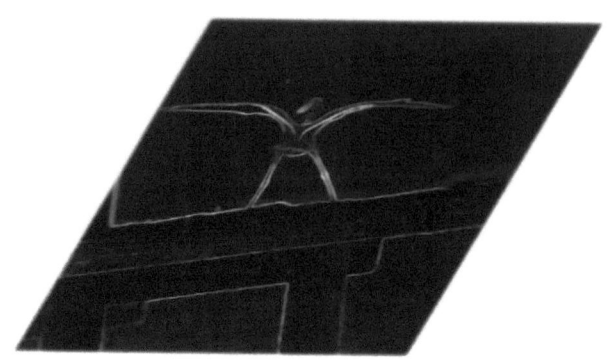

Look at the first picture in this book and you will see it and hopefully feel it. This picture did not begin that way. They were all on the ground. Only a few flying above it. And suddenly they all in a glorious pattern and choregraph took to the sky like for an audience of one on a country road just looking at them. This natural joy of being alive that birds express is one of many reasons why birds fly. They enjoy rising above everything else. It is one of the basic reasons they fly in this world.

Study the birds, even on the ground, or the limb on a tree (as I have done in years of photographing them). They spread their wings; hop around and dance to the rhythms of

nature's songs. It is like they create their own music, and dance to their own song. And they can be romantic. They give us a peak into their feathers of romance with striking displays of sounds and moves that rival the human's tango and the best of our ballet dancers. They take their courtship rituals of love and romance seriously. And it pays off—for once mated for many species, hardly anything separates them from a lifetime together: Walking together; working together; eating together; flying together; mating together; raising together; guarding one another; navigating this vast complicating world together. Birds have long learned they cannot survive alone. They look out for one another. When they see danger, they alert the others. It's one of the lessons they can teach us.

Together in Our World makes things Better.

Among the birds are species—wondrously witty, wise; with wings designed with form and freedom we do not yet understand how they do what they do. Some fly faster than most hot rod cars and they use only the force of the wind and their wings. And some with smaller wings yet fly faster than those with bigger one. There seems to be no relationship to size and speed—no combustible fuel like cars or air planes. Good clean air moves them. They hold out to us the possibility to move with natural energy without hurting the planet we live on. Indeed, they contribute to its survival. They fly with speed, grace, and beauty as if maintaining

a living and loving contract with the great winds that carry them along: The bird needs the wind to fly. The wind does not need the bird to blow. Yet the wind is always there for them if they dare to spread their wings and rise upon its power.

Yet, although they fly high, each bird takes the time to pause. Sometimes on a high mountain peak; a clef of a hill; or a ledge of a building, or on the foundation of the earth...each takes the time to stop—to take a pause to gather strength to move and fly again. They are marvels of how they use the energy of what is around them, that even helps them hatch their eggs, and bring young ones into this world.

Some like bats (not considered a bird but are exemplified here because they are one of the few animals that fly like one in three-dimensional space) are sadly associated with evil and darkness because they can effortlessly find their way in dark places where eyes are useless yet "seeing" is still necessary. So, bats "see" by using alternate abilities. They use their skills to know where to go flying at high speed in the dark. They can even tell how far an object is in

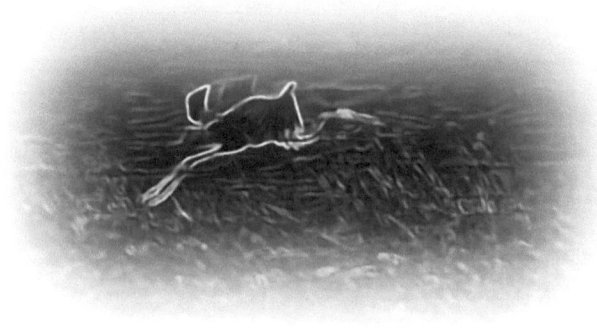

front of them. They can tell how the object is shaped, so they can go around it. And they can tell even the texture like a tree from a rock, or plants. So, they avoid hard objects while flying. They like us want to survive. How evil is that for bats? What can bats tell us? Those individuals and groups among us often given unkind depictions, bullied or treated in bad ways for being different can learn like bats and birds—to develop alternate skills for survival and just keep flying—using their incredible wings and internal GPS to keep doing what it does: Fly! Even in a dark world.

The wonderful world of birds in this world is beyond understanding. Imagine we breathe the same air. And we live in the same world. And they carry seeds of all kinds of plants life around the globe in their travels. And we eat from the plants that the birds bring to us. Imagine that! They can inspire us to reach beyond our immediate surroundings. They do it all the time.

It appears no birds exist any other place as in our world. They only exists like humans in this sphere of the universe. And their existence is critical to humans in this system as well. As we move in our lives breathing the same air and affected by the same wind in which they live as well—we often do not consider how fragile yet

interconnected is their world and ours. This connected is to the point that those in earth science who study such things find it inconceivable that our planet could function without them. There will be no pollination so vital to life of plants. There would have no plants of various kinds we depend on moving from one place to the other; that birds facilitate as they carry as they travel our world. And dare I be so bold to mention what life would be for many of us without chicken, turkey or ducks—economically as well? What can we learn here? We move

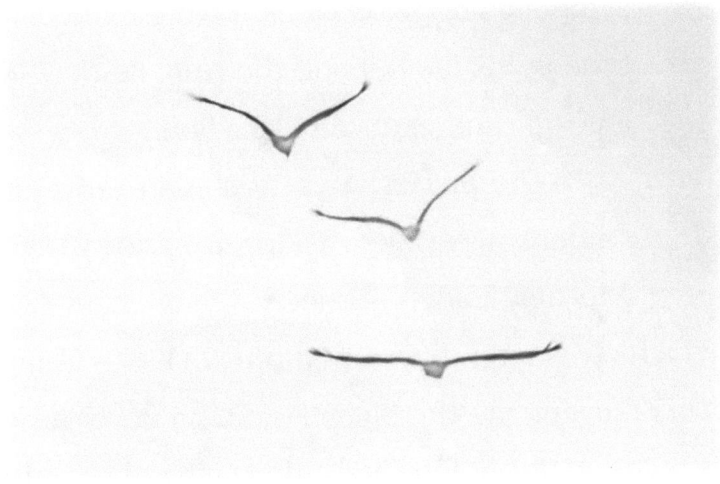

through life not realizing that we are more than blessed with their beauty— bewildered by their sounds and songs, bolstered by their sacrifice that feed us and make our lives possible in so many ways. And for all their tireless daily work they do at no wages from us—they communicate and signal to each of us only that we do our part to protect their space—their home and ours—this little speck call Earth in the universe in which so many shares so much—so together. They call us in so many ways to understanding the interconnected ecosystems that can be transformed to a critical social understanding—so we lay aside the often "ego" that produces so many conflicting "tribal" attitudes among our species. They call us in song, sound and even science to this critical interdependency of our world—living with nature's constant ever ending nudge to get along with each other and our world—at least to try—if only because our survival depends on a designed system that must work together on every level. Our survival on this earth depends on it. The birds know this. They signal that humans must know it too: *We fly together, or not at all.*

Beyond Survival

But in the wonderful world of birds, I must point out is it is not always about the grand drama of science and survival. That is basic and must be considered. However, we employ our feathered friends in many other ways that often go unnoticed. For example, in communication we draw on them to express human thoughts and characteristics that would be dry and unimpactful without them. We turn to them to express our thoughts and ideas—communicating meaning to one another. For example, when Mohamad Allie wanted to express his style of boxing and intended impact in the ring, he appealed to other creatures in memorable historical fashion. He expressed to the world his personal manner in the ring: "**I**

move like a butterfly 'and sting like a bee" and we understood what he meant—and more so over his life as he began to display these symbolic characteristics. I would add—over time in his life outside the ring, he flew like an eagle and endured like a lion.

In the Sixties, as a freshman university student, I recalled asking a national Black Panther leader –Stokely Carmichael—who came as a guest speaker at the University which I was attending. I inquired what was behind the selection of the panther as symbolic of his movement –the *Black Panther.* I never forgot his answer: "*The panther*" he said to me, '*is an animal that hardly would come at you unless it perceived that it has been cornered; with no place else to go. You corner it—it will come at you! The panther will never play dead as some other animals do."* Stokely and I came to civil rights issues in the volatile sixties from two different places. He a national political activist leader, and I an obscure evangelical student of the Bible and a preacher—dealing with matters of conflict of the soul among all peoples—still do today. But I understood deeply his unusual descriptive reply for his activist approach. He had in his description of the panther rapped up the challenges and divide the history of civil rights leadership in America and what his perspective and approach to his response and leadership was going to be—and believed demanded at the time. He was motivated by his understanding of the magnificent creature—the black panther they will fight back when cornered.

We say sometimes *"crazy like a fox;" "sing like a sparrow" "fly like an eagle"; "gentle as a dove;" "talk like a parrot."* Seems like every small town and big cities have a sport team with the name of an animal or a bird, like say the *Seattle Seahawks,* and the *Miami Dolphins* and so many others. We draw on them in many ways for their characteristics we admire in them or aspire to be. It is nothing new, of course, as Archeologists have even discovered Egyptian inscriptions dated over three Thousand years ago, mentioning invading armies captured *"like birds ensnared in a net."* And in ancient Philistines through excavations, they have uncovered a culture with abundance of pottery featuring display of birds—especially "birds looking backwards" (Modern Scholar, A *History of Ancient Israel,* Professor, Eric H. Cline, George Washington University, 2006). From ancient of time they have provided us with opportunity to communicate in words, characteristics, and even culture that enhanced our understanding of life. They communicate to us in many ways; that help us communicate more effectively with each other as well.

This book although grounded in research of various birds and other flying creatures is metaphoric in its approach. It draws on perceived characteristics of birds and other creatures to gain insights into successful living. Flying is use as a metaphor of life and action, attitudes, moving through life. I believe how birds fly—how other creatures do what they do all around us can give us insights how we can not only survive but thrive.

I love birds. The oldest photo I have of myself is about 4 years old wearing a tailored suite with a tie half the size of chest—but I remember thinking it was special because it was not an ordinary tie. It had a bird imprinted on it. Later, I acquired two young pigeons excited to raise them in a little cage I built. I did not know how fast they reproduced and was unprepared as I had to keep building larger cages. After raising to fifty pigeons there was no more space in our limited back yard to house them, so I had to begin to distribute to others to raise. The process though that span some years of my boyhood life—left a lasting impression. I never got over the mystery of seeing them fly away in the distance until you can no longer see them. They would be gone for hours—sometimes all the hours of daylight. But each evening just before dark you can see them coming and circling nearby then landing nearby on our neighbor's roof. Then each in turn on the nearby fence to the cage. It was like a daily coming home ritual with each flight and step preplanned. Then one by on in the narrow cage door. Then for a moment those that stayed home on their eggs, will get some time to exit the cage and fly, before darkness falls. Some days I would have my doubts if they would come back home when they take their flight. I would wonder where and how far they travelled. And I would wonder how they know how to find their way home. To this day I never knew how they did it. But I know this, the process of observing and taking care of all these pigeons—seeing them fly together, taking care of their young and sharing the responsibilities together from eggs to flight, and always coming back home—demonstrated a certain constancy or rhythm of life that can settle one's soul; inspire one's life. Pigeons taught me many things about life involving companionships, communication and community. I believe birds and other creatures around us have much to teach us all—giving us thoughtful ideas for successful living—to beat the odds, on the ground level and then fly above it.

Each chapter of this book presents a broad theme from the world of birds with specific application or lessons for successful living from their world and behavior. I must again point out this approach is illustrative or symbolic. It is not the result of any scientific research but just the observation of a professional photographer; a lover of these creatures and some of what I have learned along the way. I am also guided by the ancient prophets; including Jesus Christ who would often appeal to nature to express vital truth for all of us. For example, Jesus once compared His life on Earth to be like *"birds of the air have nests, but the Son of Man had*

no place to lay His head" as recorded in Luke 9:58. He used the common birds to express His uncommon life. I have had difficulty with this since my early Sunday School days: I could not understand how could he not have a place to lay His head when my Sunday School teacher kept teaching us that He made this world? In selecting the photography for this book, a bird—a hawk I photographed help me to understand perhaps the meaning of this teaching. I was traveling on highway 27 in Florida (May 2018) and saw a nest. It was high on a wooden pole about 30 feet up. I stopped to take a photo of this nest. In my line of sight, I saw what looked like a small dove. As it came closer as I took photos, I realized it was a large hawk heading for its nests—the same one I was photographing. The young ones in the nest became active as she approaches.

It was not until later viewing of this beautiful hawk as I followed its distant trail to the very nest, I was photographing that I notice two informative features of this bird as seen in the photograph above: (1) That bird – the hawk was carrying a large bark of a tree. And (2) In the middle of its nest the head of a young hawk—like literally *waiting in the wings.*

I have photographed many hawks fishing and taking its catch to feed their young. This was the first time capturing a hawk with building materials to secure its nest for her growing young. Both can be noticed in the photograph here. It was flying with it in the grip of its claws from a long distance to continuing building this nest to protect its young. To be honest,

this event photographing this hawk yet building its nests with its young in it, help me to understand and reflect on this bible question that puzzled me as a boy in Sunday School. Why did Jesus said birds they have "*nests*" but He had "*no place to lay His head?*" The world is a big place, He said He made it, how could He  not have a place—was my thinking. The message from this nest and this bird with the building materials carried on its winged body, I learned and observed: **He made this world for the birds and other living creatures and not for Himself. The materials "fit for Him"—are not available here. And the quality required for His abode would be beyond what can be produced here.** The materials for the birds to build their nests are ample provided here. But He was from Heaven—the only place with the materials suitable for a place He "lay His head." He came here to redeem and not to rest or to reside. Like a bird though, He returned to that place and is building a heavenly nest with heavenly materials which cannot be found or exist here. John 14 began to make sense not just simple that He said "*I go to prepare a place for you*" but why he had to do so. The building materials could not be used. He could not build a place for himself by sending His disciples to a local hardware store. Nothing in this world was "fit" for Him to lay His head. It's a lesson from the hawk that at least gave me some personal understand of perhaps what Jesus meant. The materials here was not fit for a heavenly Person—a God like him. Could not rest here. Just a thought from the hawk.

I like traveling on country roads with open fields with different livestock; perhaps because I grew up helping my dad who raised livestock of different kinds (bulls, cattle, goats, sheep, pigs...). I once saw a field filled with large bulls. And in the middle of it all was a most elegant, beautiful bird sitting without a care in the world on the back of a bull—a massive powerful animal who with a single whip of its tail can crush this little bird into flying feathers. What prevents this from happening is rooted in the relationships between the big bull and the little bird; such powerful destructive force is restrained. And the little birds stand on the back of the bull well within reach of its powerful tail  without fear. Indeed, it's a relationship of value. For despite the power of the bull's tail it does not have the reach to protect its massive body from unwanted nuisance of gnats, flies, and other insects trying to get a piece of the bull. But not for this harmless yet fearless little Cattle Egret, that simple wanted to rest on its massive body—and with it giving us a real-life drama of nature's version of *"beauty and the beast"*—sharing with us nature's intersection of tremendous power and peace all in one—contras and yet community—something humans often have difficulty with; distinct yet seemingly indistinguishable with one another. I had passed by this event for some two miles before I realized I needed to stop and returned to capture this common yet unusual yet powerful teachable moment from nature's creatures. Creatures seemingly unaware of the unlikely relationship among humans where the powerful often desire to dominate the weak and vulnerable. Those often hit with the stereotype like that of *"a bull in a china shop"*—the bull being cast as an uncontrollable power should reconsider from this picture of calm and control—the bull resting on the earth and the bird resting on the bull—power and poise—privilege and pleasure:

It is quite a different picture from the bulls we often see for entertainment. But who am I kidding to even attempt to describe the powerful and real symbols and lessons for humans in this picture? They tell us about our world. Its fragile existence and interdependence—in their own way they give us early warnings—even with their lives they do—to identify dangers before they hit us. They are here to fundamentally teach us ways to live. How to work together—how to live together-how to interact with one another—how one species would take care of another in ways they could not do on their own and in ways that is necessary for their survival. How could we not learn from them? How could we not understand a peaceful perspective of paradise from the precepts of the Prophet in his analogy: "The wolf will live with the lamb, the leopard will lie down with the goat, the calf and the lion and the yearling together; and a little child will lead them. A place if one can imagine where animals that devour each other find peace. A place where predator and the prey hanging out with one another.

They in our time teach us the sensitivity and vulnerability of our planet. They are an early warning to us of things to come if we do not change how we use this planet resources. They are a part of it as well. They are all like the "*canary in the coal mine*" once used by coal miners as an early warning of rising toxic gasses—the canary would become sick or die giving the minors an early warning to save themselves. Although, sensitive chemical instruments have replaced the need for canaries—the role of the early warnings to humans on this planet has not changed. In so many ways they yet warn us if we pause to look and listen. And regrettable, there are many important species to our planet could soon be extinct as their early warning systems for protection against human's the onslaught of increased poachers targeting their existence for pleasure and profit until they are gone.

Birds in the Bible

I must also admit, in my research for this book I turned to the Bible and was intrigue how our feathered friends fly through its pages from Genesis to Revelations; landing at various points in its narrative to teach and illustrate important lessons for life. For example, they filled the heavens in creation. Consider without them the sky would be empty of life: "And God said 'Let the water teem with living creatures. **And let birds fly above the earth across the vault of the sky**" (Genesis 1:20). It was a bird—a dove that failed to return to the Ark after making several trips that signal to Noah it was safe to leave the ark (Genesis 8). When Elijah fled for his life among barren places ravens came to his aid; sent by God to feed him (1 Kings 17). Isaiah said those who trust in God will "**mount up on wings as eagles**" (40:31). And Jesus who was a master teacher in the New Testament narrative using earthly illustrations for heavenly meanings invited us to: **"Look at the birds of the air; they do not sow or reap or store away in barns, and yet your heavenly Father feeds them ...(Matthew 6:26).**

Later He asked the disciples along the same theme of His compassionate care: Are not two sparrows sold for a penny? Yet not one of them will fall to the ground outside your Father' care (Matthew 10:29). And He used the dove to symbolize how

His followers should be as they move among the unbelieving world: "Shrewd as snakes and as innocent as doves" (v.16). And perhaps the greatest symbolic example of a bird in the Bible is one representing the Holy Spirit would be the power in the movement of Jesus. Here the Spirit is represented by a lowly dove.

"Oh, that I had the wings of a dove!

I would fly away and be at rest.

I would flee far away and stay in the desert...(Psalm 55:6-7).

The ravens And the Holy Spirit came in the form of a dove to establish the Christian church. Their characteristics teaches us character. Their abilities advance ours. Their work gives us wisdom. Their morning songs lifts our spirits all day long. They encourage us to dream dreams with the sky as the limit. They are in the Old Testament to teach Israel the way they ought to go, and in the New Testament sermons of Jesus to teach us lessons—to help us understand and apply. They function seamlessly in both worlds of land and air to teach us that we as well can function in both world that of the physical and the spiritual as well. When the Palmist was overwhelmed with his troubles—tired in his body and soul, his sprit wanted to take flight: *"Oh that I had wings like a dove I would fly away and be at rest"* he said in one of his songs. The Psalmist quite possible could have been using to *"be at rest"* as a metaphor of death as the Christian's ultimate rest. In which case, this desire to *"fly away"* would be one of the greatest flight on wings anyone can take—the last flight to soar to glory—the bird becomes the ultimate metaphor of both a positive life—flying towards death as the ultimate point of rest from the turbulent winds that often comes our way in this life.

I was standing one day contemplating in an opened field. The awareness of being at a grave site lost—looking up into the sky. There was solace falling down with rays of sunlight unfiltered by nature's clouds or human dusts. Looking up filled with sunlight left no room for fear or sadness. That day seems to be the clearest day I have ever seen or experience—it looked more like a mirror with sky reflecting sky. As I was caught up in this uplifting scene a thought came rushing into my mind and heart and I said out loud—although no one was around to hear but God: **"This is a good day for flying."** I felt I was flying far above what the place I was standing represented. This though and experience—looking at the clear open sunny sky, became the creative source of this book: Why do birds fly.

A Bird's View:

I cannot imagine what it's like for humans stuck on the ground and do not get to see things the way we do—from the top. If they can only learn to be like us they can fly way above the cares of the earth—for cares cannot fly—they cannot follow—they cannot keep up when you do.

More lessons to come...

1 "Wings"

"In a World filled with People, only some want to fly. Isn't that crazy?
—Seal— (Crazy 1991)

On its face, it seems trite to say birds fly because they have wings. Yet, it is true. This is one of the first and basic lesson we can learn from our feathers' friends: They fly because they grow wings. They offer us a metaphor for anything humans desire to achieve in this world. You cannot fly without them. You cannot clip them and hope they are going to work for you. *If you are going to achieve something, you must first develop what it takes to do so. And the*

higher you want to fly the greater the wingspan you going to need. An eagle cannot fly on chicken wings. You want to fly like an eagle you must develop the wings of an eagle. Some of

the great truths for success are so basic yet often ignored. This is one of them. It is hard to think of people growing up without dreams. What makes the difference with those who achieve them and those who do not? Some develop the wings required to get them there and others do not. It is that basic. And there are no short-cuts.

For example, you want to be successful in school you must study. Even if you do not like to do so— you must develop the habit if you want success in higher learning. You want to be an author you must learn to write and keep writing. You want to be an actress or actor you must work hard at developing the skills required. It is the first law of human flight. You must develop wings.

I use the words "develop wings" carefully and selectively. Because, in the metaphor of wings I believe each person is born with wings. Each person has within them the seeds of greatness—the potential to rise above whatever station they find themselves—the potential to raise above one's down circumstances. It is like the birds having wings—of mind body and soul.

It is that real life begins when one discovers the wings-set they were given—develop them to fly. In this sense, every single person no matter their class, religion, race or creed or any other of the many classifications place on a person. What is important is discovering your wings you were given—develop them day by day and you will experience that moment when you can use them to fly—when you do—keep flying.

To fly develope your **wings.**

Each person has wings to fly. *By this I mean each person has been given an ability to reach beyond themselves and develop into something new each day.* Each person has "wings"—they may yet be unknown, but they are there. The main function for living is to discover the wings you have been given and fly.

A Bird's View:

In my nest

I wondered why I am not flying the world like the rest

I see them far away riding on air, but with lingering fear if I could get there

I dream of all the things I will like to be—all the things I will like to do and see... Until I noticed I was enveloped with wings—one on each side of me.

So, I took to the sky and soared as high as I could be, with the wings discovered in me.

We Were Made to Fly
We All Have Wings,
Use Them and
Rise Up!

Few Faithful Flyers From the Bible

David

David long before he became one of the great kings of Israel demonstrated his ability to use the wings he had. As a boy he had his way with a sling slot hurling smooth stones with astonishing accuracy. For young David his *wings* became his sling slot and a stone. His countrymen lived in fear of Goliath. He was a giant warrior of the Philistines who terrorized Israelites. No one dare challenge Goliath. He was in a class of worriers of his times who stood strong and never lost a battle. Moreover he used his standing and strength to shame Israel and their God. One day young David heard one of these shameful ranting that struct fear in the hearts of his people. His will was stirred to do something. All he had was his sling-shot and his smooth stones as his weapon against a giant. But with these two wings the sling-shot and a stone he soured to unexpected heights and the

To Fly Spread the Wings you Have

giant came falling down. David was not the only lad who used sling-shots to propelled stones. But his wings was his extraordinary ability to combine force with accuracy; with one strike the giant fell.

Wings are not items which can be borrowed. You own them. They can be used against all the giants that stand in your way of success. Fly! Like little David did against a big giant and won.

Moses

I must be brief as we have considered Moses more extensively before. But he is worth keeping in mind from the perspective of a bible example. When he was called to deliver his people he felt he was not up to the task—that he had nothing to make a difference. He felt like a bird who flew from Egypt to Mount Sinai, and since lost his "wings" to return. But God attempted to show him that was not so. That all this time he carried his wings in his hand in the form of a rod—every day. He had his wings. And that was all he needed to fly out of Egypt and take his people with him.

Limitations of all stripes has but one message: You cannot do this or that so don't even try. Wings answer *watch me fly!*

Ester

Ester was unique in the way she used her wings. For Ester as far as we know what Ester had was her beauty. As far as we can tell from the Bible narrative she had gotten to her position of prominence as a princess solely because of the beauty God gave her. It appeared from the narrative that she was so beautiful that the King did not seek to question or to know that she was a foreigner—a Jew. He saw only her beauty. Other women often used their extraordinary beauty for personal pleasure and power. Not so Ester. With the wings of her extraordinary beauty God gave her and with it she soured. For when like Egypt her people's survival was threatened her beauty enable her to approach the kind on behalf of her people, and she won their release from annihilation.

Each person needs to discover their wings. God gave each person the ability to fly—to accomplish even far beyond their own expectations—to fly. But they need to first discover their wings—their spirit—if they want to soar beyond the level on which they stand.

Everyone is beautiful in their own way. But let's be honest. There are people who like other given talents or abilities handed down to them among them are people who are incredibly beautiful. The Songs of Songs in the Bible stands as a testimony—of biblical proof of this. For it is a Book and a Song about beauty. So what I am saying here. If you are blessed with beauty. If opportunity comes your way much easier because of it. Like Ester use it to help others with the power that it gives you to get attention. There is a saying (and I say this in all honesty to make an important point): *Beauty is but skin deep, but ugliness is to the bones*. If God blessed, you with extraordinary beauty, own it and use it to fly like Ester to help others less fortunate than you. If you use it only to fly for yourself it becomes ugly to the bones. It is the reason why Ester is one of the most beautiful lady in the Bible.

A little boy was interrupting class very often with his questions for the teacher. After several days of his interruption, his teacher put a stop to it and told him in front of the class to sit down and never stand again. To the amazement of his class mate he did so. He had never listened to any such instruction before. So outside of class they got a hold of him and ask him how was he able to stay seated throughout the class. He told them his secret: "I was standing up inside!" His wings was his resolve to stay standing, albeit inside.

2 "Will"

In research for this book, I did more than taking photos of birds. I spoke to people who knew a lot more about birds than I do. I studied their behavior. I try to understand a little of their world. I love to observe them on site in their natural habitat or surroundings like in the fields. However, I also find it very beneficial having taken many photos of a bird to then study their behavior through still photographs. (A good photographer can see motion in a still frame—sometimes more than a video). It is like doing the impossible—freezing time just enough to study it. It enables the photographer to understand or "see" what goes into a decisive moment that often gets lost in the flow of action—say in a video. So, I learn much from looking at still photographs. Now different ones can look at a photograph and see different characteristics. That is natural. In the combination of different views can also be found increase knowledge and understanding.

In this photo above I see a striking illustration of the second important step in learning to fly: **One must have more than wings to fly. They must have the "will" to do so.** They must have like birds the natural **"will"** to fly. Among hundreds of photographs, I wanted to find a bird that represented that all important human trait necessary for achievement and success—the "will" to succeed—the will to fly. This is express in different ways in different cultures and diverse expressions. But here I would say it is **an emotional, mental, or spiritual energy to do something. It is that internal initial spark that gets the fire of life and action going—that gets one reaching to the sky.**

For example, here is this adult *limpkin* (in the photo above)—something inside that limpkin moves it to the point of no return and as a lesson to us, notice that it does so without its wings. First it had a certain dependence. It knows that it can depend on its wings to carry out the flight it is about to take. Otherwise it would not take such an action knowing it would fall in the lake below. But the action of the flight begins inside of the bird—in the "will" of the bird. Look at the committed angle of its legs. Its will is translated to her legs (seen in their forward angle) even before it opens its wings, her whole-body weight is already in the direction she wants to fly. It is already on the move. It is already *"all in"* or all committed to flying. It is already at a point of no return. If it does not fly, it falls into the water beneath her. It is taken to that point through share "will" and not wings because although wings are necessary to fly, unless there is a will behind the wings you cannot **get going**.

Movement towards any goal begins with the will and often is sustained by it to succeed. It is as important as wings in learning to fly. Like this limpkin bird above, clearly committed to flight before it even opens its wings because its weight to a large degree is no longer supported by its legs. I looked to see if I can find even a slight opening of its wings—to "hedge its bets" but could not see such at that decisive moment. The limpkin had confidence in her ability to fly. It demonstrated it by its commitment to the sky. What comes first—the wings or the will? A young bird attempting to learn to fly could not do so without the will to fly. It is one of the most distinguishing elements in success and achievement. I do not know which one comes first. What I do know is that you need both. One without the other lands you on the ground and keep you there.

It is said a picture is worth a thousand words, so I do not have to say much here. This bird—this limpkin simple acted. It started its flight without depending aerodynamically on the science of it wings—not to initiate its flight. It was committed to do so by its will even before its physical attributes became linked to its will to fly.

If a person does not believe in themselves, it is not likely they are going to fly to achieve much. One cannot achieve beyond the power of their will would allow. They will soon fall apart despite all the wings-ability they have. But when strong wings linked up with a strong will to accomplish something the sky becomes the limit. How many times we have looked at a game—statistically the players match up. We know the players and the physical abilities they

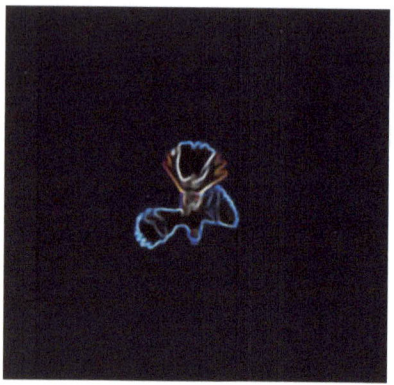

bring to the game but confronted with an equally fit opponent it comes down to which team has the **will to win**. And it is not simple momentary. It must be sustained throughout the game if you want success. That internal energy of the "will" is what get you going. It is also what takes you through the clouds and the storm, and the rain. It takes more than wings to keep you going. It also takes will to keep you flying.

A Bird's View:

When I was a chick, I had so much will and desire to fly,

But I had no wings, so I stayed in my nest all the while.

As time passed though, my wings began to grow.

But then I still could not fly, because my will and desire did subside

So, I stayed there and rest until my parents pushed me out of this comfortable nest.

And somewhere between that high secure nest and the hard earth below where I could fall and die I quickly found my will to fly.

The Willing Bird in the Bible

The very first bird mention in the bible is found in Genesis....It was after Noah had built the ark and all the animals two by two had gotten in. Then the rain had stopped, and the flooding was over but Noah could not see any land on which to get the whole grew back on dry ground. So he called on a dove to fly out the Ark and note when the earth was dry enough so that the animals would be safe to walk out of the ark. The bird flew out on it renascence and the Bible narrative says the dove kept coming back for it found no place to land. The story of this dove is, its will. It never gave up flying out of the ark until it found land. And that is how the rest of the crew was safe. It was in addition to the will of God, the will of a little bird.

The Earnest Eagle

Development of the Will

The Eagle which is the highest-flying bird in the sky did not start out that way. Their earliest tendencies of a baby eagle is to stay in the next as long as they could. Looking at the world from tin their nests was way high enough. The world outside the safety of their nest seems daunting to the young eagles. The parent most important task other than rigorously hunting for food to keep them alive at a certain point turned to the important task is to teach them to go out on their own and find their own food. But their first inclination for these young eagles were to stay in the safety of the nest as long as they could. But sound eagle parenting would have none of this.

So the parent eagles in different ways start to develop the will of these young nesting eagles. One of the striking ways it was do so is to shatter the nests in such a way as to make it almost inhabitable or unconfutable for these young eagles. Their "will" in nurtured to fly out the nects by deliberately making the next uncomfortable for them (Deuteronomy 32:11). These birds that would someday fly to heights of any birds can, first struggled to get out of their nests. No matter how large and ingeniuous their wings they would never fly relying on their comfortable surroundings. Not when the sky is the limit. Mom and pop eagles knows that. So they first shatter their nests. If that fails to work to get them even to try to fly, they then take the next step to literally pick them up and take to the sky let them go so they learn to spread their wings and fly. The parent eagleswould not let the young crash to the ground. But would repeat this action until their young learn to spred their wings and reach to the sky instead of falling to the ground. After they developed this will, they shakes off dependency and takes on the sky.

Why do people fall, say from their diet? Or, fall from other goals they set out to achieve? They did not develop their will. Achievements are not always about one's physical attributes. Physical attributes such as talents can take you far. There is a level of achievements that every serious athlete knows that only the will survive.

I saw an old man getting out of a passenger seat next to me. He did so in painstakingly slow motion. I looked at him as I waited for my turn. His body frail and slow from the relentless flow from the challenge of time. Except for his eyes seems they were filled with grit and determination. He had a look of defiance fighting against legs calling him to stay put. But his eyes--the windows of the soul filled with the will to get to that waiting wheel chair held by another. What started as an observation of slow painful progress—one look into his eyes and not his frailer body that hardly moving, sees a will to success to reach from his passenger seat to a waiting wheel chair but inches away. In his eyes filled with years of determination each as they wait respected a will to beat the odds—still struggling—still flying high after all these years. It is more than the natural will to live. It is the will to succeed at living—not just existing. It is as Jesus said "I come that you might have life and have it more abundantly" (John 10:10). It is the will to want more out of life than what it naturally give. The will to take it—use it as a precious gift to give more back to it. Like a life stream unrestricted by meanderings, rocks, or passing debris. Often in a competitive game where it is obvious the opponents seemed equally matched. Yet one stands out in that day—in that moment with their will to win soaring beyond the equal abilities of opportunities to succeed. One distinguished themselves by the sheer will. I was looking at the Summer Olympics in Los Angelis, I was called to the TV to see marathon runner Gabriela Andersen-Schiess. She literally dragged her body to get to the finish line, seen around the world. By her own account said it was the will to get to the finish that made for that dramatic finish moment in the Summer Olympics of 1984, one of the great Olympic finishes in its history—by share will she became an inspiration to many and soured to hights.

She became an inspiration to many to know that everyone may not have all the ability to physically but often the will takes them through.

Where there is a Will, Wings will Follow

3 "Way"

> *"Birds seems to always know where they are going. Humans need to catch up!"*

So, you have (1) **wings**—those unique abilities inside of you. Some are latent—yet to be discovered. Hardly, one is found that does not open doors to another—a discovery available at any age in the course of life.

And you have (2) **will**— that inner spark—that inner fire as unique as your fingerprint or your genetic code. It can be lit or smothered by others but never transferred. It is there. Let no one keep you down. It is yours: Your drive; your zeal; your desire to act; your motivation to achieve—the sacred space between who you are and you can be. And it's up to you. Like a bird, it is what occupy that space that makes it spread its wings and fly to where it wants to be. But, in that space, how do you know where to go? How do you discover your path? How do you find your (3) **way?** (In the photo above I saw two birds pouched on my weather vein. Each facing opposite directions. I wondered would it help them to know which way to take. I concluded no, for they had their own direction already written in their own language inside).

14

If you like a bird is ready to fly, how do you know the direction to the sky?

This chapter is about lessons from the birds I have picked up along the way—learning to fly from the course they take. These I called "bird clues."

"There are Clues to the Course."

There are many surprising characteristics about birds. As a species they have feathers—long legs, short legs, long beaks short beaks, wings that defy present aerodynamic technology. It would have been by itself a valiant act just to be able to soar to fly to the sky. But is so many astonishing ways they do much more than that. First, they seem to fly with a plan. Their movements and directions seem never to be random, counterproductive or obituary. They fly with poise and purpose. They all occupy space upon the earth with a personal sense of belonging. Some like the rooster seems to take charge of the day—calling out to each within its voice including humans. to rise and shine. Even Jesus was very much aware of their skills to remind one of His wayward disciple Peter.

I was awakened each morning by a rooster with a distinct sound and at a consistent time each day growing up. His timing and mine did not jell. He was to early for me. But I knew it was just doing its job. For it had a distinct sound. And there were more roosters around, but you never hear all the rooster sounding at once. It seems to have been an assigned task selected among the roosters clan. And who can compete with the proud peacock weather among birds or human with the way they can occupy their spaces—with an unabashed sense of belonging—personal pride and dignity? What among birds determine their way? What give them their obvious sense of belonging and direction in their interaction with the land, the sea and the sky? I have found what I call clues—or "hints" as to how birds find their **Way to fly** and show us humans how to do the same.

Clue One

One of the primary "clues" I have observed is bird's physical characteristics determine the course they take. It is almost like a "calling" in a bird's life. For example, Birds with long legs and beaks inhabit places they can use them; like in shallow ponds. Homing pigeons incredible find their way home from faraway places with such precision that still from ancient of times baffle scientists as to how they do it. They like other birds function according to the attributes or inherent "tools" they were given or developed. Others, although look the same would never find their way home without such ability. They do so because they have the ability to do so. Other birds would die if they were foolish enough to try. They do not. The seems to have a sense of their personal attributes and are willing to use them with a sense of purpose of that was what they were meant to do. That is an important lesson to learn in finding your path—knowing the way to take.

The hawks and the eagles fly high because they have the physical attributes required to do so. They are not ducks. But the ducks can hold their own in ponds and rivers more than eagles can. Eagles cannot waddle like ducks. Ducts cannot fly like eagles. Each do the max what they are given tools to accomplish. That is the secret: Knowing your unique abilities using expanding them to the max. There are bird's species like the crane with beaks that are long to grab shells below the surface of ponds and shallow rivers, as well as strong enough to crack the shells they find there. And others with gentle beaks fit only to handle worms and other delicacies they feed on and feed their little ones. There are birds with wings that looks like other birds yet just beneath the feathers are anatomically-physically distinct and

incredible versatile. Some birds' wings are designed for swift maneuvers—and hovering like the hummingbird—while others are designed for high speed like the peregrine falcon that can reach speeds over 230 miles per hour while diving for its meal—achieving the fastest speed of any animal on earth. Only the golden eagle comes in at a close second with speeds up to 200 miles per hour. Other birds are gifted not for speed but maneuverability or for gliding gently the winds with little or no efforts in unbelievably efficiency with little energy—yet much control. I have found (in my non-scientific observations) a rigorous consistency between their physical attributes which then demine their WAY.

What is the point of this as a clue as to how humans determine their "way" or their destiny or purpose in life? It is that eagles could not fly like eagles do on chicken wings. Each person to find fulfillment in their life follows the pattern of their feathers—their features that lies beneath them. Then us them to the max to function in this world. So, to be successful at any level you must first find the answer to the following questions: What unique attributes like the different wings of birds do you have? How high will they let you go? Where will they let you fly? That is, what physical attributes do you have beneath your skin that enable you to win in what you want to achieve? It is the way of the birds. The rooster crows at a time and

with a unique sound that says, "get up!" It is how it was "wired." They are not song birds. What kind of bird are you? What kind of wings do you have? What are you "wired" to be—that seems so natural to you? Not what you are doing, but what do you desire to do or to be? That is the primary clue as to how you find your way in the open sky.

For example, when I was growing up, I soon found in me a desire to figure things out. It was so dominant in me I often got in trouble with my parents. I once opened a radio looking for the person talking inside. I needed to know who was doing the talking inside of it. I was not old enough to know this could not be—no one was there. It is perhaps the reason I got a degree in communication theory—still trying to discover who's talking inside. I was just responding to what was in me. I opened a clock because I wanted to know what made it move, and got into good trouble for it. Weather it is a toy like a top that spin until it could not spin any more. It was still spinning in my head with a question what made this top go and what made it stop. My Sunday School teacher told me God is everywhere. So, I went home and crawled to the furthest point under my mother's big bed and curled up in the dark corner said to God: "See if you can find me now!" Where does these inherent urgings and dispositions come from? To this day from God, Genes, or nature I still do not know for sure. I find I could remember a complex concept for a lifetime, but somehow have an embarrassing problem of remembering a person's name within seconds after they told me. When my wife and I would go to an important function. She stayed close to me as I met guests and faithfully nudged me and whispered their names. Names seems to take flight like some birds, while more complex concepts come back like homing pigeons.

My mom wanted me to be a Taylor and sent me to learn from one. I was bored. I begged my mom to let me do something else. I was never happy threading needles into cloth. On the other hand, I was at home in an appliance shop—there after school I was excited to learn what made a toaster gets hot and pop up the bread after it was done. What made an iron gets hot and then took wrinkles out of cloths—even before I was a teenager. I was at home learning what makes things work. To this day I still enjoy this pursuit as I spent the time researching for this book—considering Why do birds fly? But of course, it is more of a mix of the physical attributes of birds towards a more metaphorical understanding in its application. I am fascinated with what I find to be a mysterious relationship between humans and other creatures. For example, why do they do so many things we cannot? This is something that often puzzle me. After all, did we not come from them? How could this be? How can an elephant hear miles away and we cannot hear someone we love right in front of us? I am just asking. I am still trying to figure it out.

Poise

Passion

Purpose

Take the time to listen to what your body is allowing you to be. What is your mind physically wired you to achieve? There you will find your way. Do you have wings to glide to  your destination, or do you have the ability to maneuver—get around difficult situations—a problem solver. Are you built for speed? Do you find that some things come easy and quick for you to figure out? In what areas? Technical? Relationships? Political? Social? Sports? Language? People? Business? The sky is the limit, but you need to know the wings you have to fly there. It is the most important clue to success. This is another clue that the birds give us. It is like God asked Moses before He sent him to Egypt to deliver his people: "What do you have in your hand?" In Moses case it was but a shepherds' rod. But it was what came in handy in Egypt. Ask yourself what do you have unique to you?

What is the point I am making with this clue? The point of this: We love to say to others **"you can do anything you set your mind too."** The truth is, not **"anything."** That statement might be good motivational tool for some, but it is not based on real life. Birds know that. They live with it every day. It does not bother them. They function in a real world not a make-believe one. The little humming bird cannot fly like the eagle. The eagle cannot hover like the humming bird. Each bird interacts with their world according to the unique physical attributes they have. Humans function of this basic rules of nature as well. The challenge is to use to the fullest extent their inherent abilities they have been given weather as some believe by God or developed through nature. The rule and the clue they give is the same. It is the age-old question it was said that God asked Moses who was reluctant to go and deliver his people from Egypt: "Moses what you have in your hand?" All he had was a piece of stick. That stick which was his own became symbolic of all the resources available to him like the wings of a bird to fly: Get out of Egypt. Get away from the things that keep you down.

The same clue comes from the ducks. They are not hawks. They cannot plunge into the waters at high speed, but they know how to navigate and stay above it. They know how to lead their young in a precise line—staying together despite contrary currants to find their way to the shores.

Clue 2

Another important "clue" to understanding how birds find their "**Way**" is to discover what seems to be an incredible **contentment** within their feathers. Their seem to be among birds a general contentment with the abilities they have. Birds are good polka players. They know how to use the hand they are dealt to their maximum benefit. By "contentment" I do not mean content to do nothing. It is a unique kind of **active contentment**. A contentment to **act to the max** of their ability without allowing any physical restrictions or limitations compared

to other birds prevent them from doing whatever they were given to do through their unique abilities. The ostrich is the largest bird. It has wings not capable of lifting its weighty body. So, it uses it wings to stable its body and no other bird is as fast as the ostrich is on land—gaining over forth miles per hour on land.

Humans tend to live in a competitive world of always comparing themselves with other human beings. And when they do not measure up some can fall apart—even to the extreme of ending their lives. Birds do not do that. There are no signs that the hummingbird is frustrated that it cannot fly like an eagle or move as fast as the hawk. Perhaps for the simple reason that a hummingbird which seems to have the ability to stay perfectly still in its space while its wings is in rapid motion; up to over 75 beats a second in some species. The eagle and many other

flying birds cannot come close. There are no contest among birds of who can flap their wings the fastest, or fly the highest, or among the vast differences of abilities. But each seems to

be "content" to the max in what they are capable of doing. Humans seems to be constantly comparing themselves with others to judge their achievements or lack of it. Not so the birds. They seem to have this ability to compare themselves with their own given potential rather than with other birds. I could not imagine a group of pigeons convening a high-level conference to deal with how to fly like eagles or sing like sparrows, or go to war over their differences. They would not waist their bird life doing that. They seek to fly to the max of what their own abilities and unique gifts would allow them to do. Birds are at piece in their feathers and what inside of them. I have photographed many "lonely" birds like on a wire and astonished as to the phenomenal and variety of display and performance. One morning staying a hotel on the second level just below the level of

the power wirers seeing a bird all alone yet leaping of the power wire and using its wings to flip like on a trampoline in a beautiful display of its maneuverability. It was leaping off the wire and returning in full display its "contentment" in its abilities. These photos above are of a single bird flipping upside down using a high powered electric wire like a human trampoline.

What was amazing is there were no other birds around. And I was far away using a telephoto long lens from about 100 feet away. This bird seems to give us a clue to find our way forward by learning to dance; to be happy, to be excited about life even when no one is looking. It is like finding your way by finding what make you content when you are alone.

I do not see any behavioral indications to imagine one bird being disappointed about the size of their wings: the color of its fathers or the size of their beaks or their bodies. Some birds are "thin" like cranes and others more developed like turkeys, ostrich, or ducks, but none seems to care one way or the other as humans do. They seems in their behavior and interaction and sometimes non-interaction to be content beneath their feathers. But again, such contentment for the birds does not mean inaction or suggest the idea of settling. It suggests the ability to be "content" to focus on maximizing on what abilities they have. Their overwhelming actions and interactions are consistently focused on doing their particular part in the ecological system for its good and not fighting among themselves as to who can fly higher than the other, or build the biggest nest. Each seems to be "content" with the nests that suite them.

Those little song birds sing because each one was born with a beautiful voice. Each one discovered a unique ability among the birds family to sing, and so they sing. Sometimes it is but a lone voice among many, but it sings because that is what it was born and given the ability to do.

The question to answer is: What unique ability have you discovered within you? It may be even more that an ability. It could come like a set of ideas, thoughts beliefs you find swelling up in you. Some of the best gift does not come from the obvious physical abilities that often steal the show. Look for your abilities that exist within you. It is like the particular way you look at the world. Do not overlook the creative side of existence. These are often the abilities that get lost in the mix—your abilities beyond the physical space. There many have found clues to their destiny, simple in the things they like to do. These can be clues to your "way" your destiny and possibilities. Listen to what is singing within you and be content with this unique gift or gifts and use them to the extent you can. Follow its tune, move and dance to its rhythm. Happiness is not found in how high you can fly. It is to fly as high as your unique wings will take you. Those inner clues, or abilities, positive believe and convictions about who and what you are become the place where destiny are determined. I call them "**clues to the sky**—lessons from the birds."

I have notice in learning from birds they seems to be most comfortable doing what they were made to do. For example, I look at hawks and they love to make their nest on high. And they love to fly high in the sky for that is what they were made to do. I observe buzzards and photograph them in their natural habitat. I had the impression that all they do was to eat dead things until one day I happened upon two of them mating. And there were nothing dead about that ritual. It changed my perception of the ugly buzzards, which goes to show its hard to tell what a bird is like just by its outward features, feathers, or its usual day job. And they have the ability to mate for life which for what ever reason humans fail at well over 50% fifty percent of the time.

I have listened to the song birds in the morning, and even when the night falls—just after the sun goes down. I could not see them. They are illusive except for their songs. I heard them singing—little birds with big voices—even in the dark.

I have observed in the multitude of birds flying in different direction none seem confused as to the path they take. Some migrate from one paths of the earth to the other without any stop signs, detour directions, streets or avenues—no human GPS, and no road rage. In a clear sky where every direction seems the same, they know the way to take. Where did their navigational skills come from? What mystery lies in the heavens that speaks only to birds to find their path? If a bird can find their path in the sky we must believe there is a path for us on the Earth.

Come Rain or Shine I am Ready to Rise

In the animal kingdom it seems humans are the most helpless when it comes to navigating life on the earth. I have never heard of a bird needing drugs, or any kind of medications just to get them through the day. Birds do not need to smoke to help them fly or become dependent on any medication. They eat the things that they naturally need and are content to do so. Yet for many humans the need and desire for such can reach epidemic proportions—and many die in their use and dependency. They could not find their path. They did not know how to navigate the winds of circumstances, like the birds do.

I do not know how birds find their way in the open sky. I could not say to another on purely humanistic ground how to find their path. It is the reason why I call what I say here "clues." I look for clues. There are far too many to consider here. So, we just cover a few.

Clue 3

Clue three is that I have observed birds often would be corporation with other birds to accomplish many different tasks. Some of them even critical for their own survival. There is this tendency among certain species to complement each other to achieve certain purposes. For example, there are two species of vultures. One has the ability to spot food from quite a

distance in the sky and the other cannot. So, it fly with the one that can. But that is not the whole story. When the one that can see gets to the ground it has a problem. It's beak is not very strong, while the other that could not spot the meat has an extraordinary beak strong enough to rip apart bones. They need each other, so they work together in community to survive.

This is not an isolated phenomena in nature. Examples abounds in nature of different animals work together to attack as others working together to defend against attacks. We should never use the word "turkeys" to describe say people who representative us in congress. Because if they were truly turkeys they might work together.

4 Work

Five photographic frames taken within one second of activity for this adult hawk. *Birds work their wings off-even at play. Life in the sky is work.*

Frame 1

Frame 2

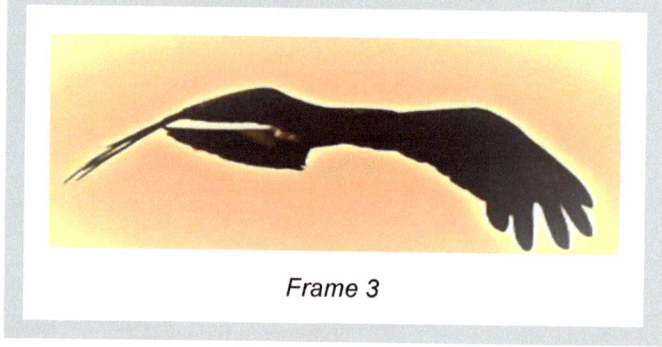

Frame 3

Frame 4

Frame 5

The fourth "w" principle for successful living as a lesson form the birds is **work**. The birds make it looks easy for sure. But on close observation flying is work. It is not free. It has a cost and it is work. The above photographs represent 5 frames of this hawk. They were captured using my SLR Nikon five frames per second shutter speed (Despite the advanced quality of cell phone photos, my camera of choice is still my Nikon Digital SLR's). Observe the verity of motion or action the bird deployed within a span of a second—involving the bird's entire body in motion—flying against the wind. Extend this motion within a second to 5 minutes, or 10 or more. Do the math of the motion and you can come to an obvious conclusion: To fly is to work—a bird cannot fly without working at it. Success at flying requires decided action towards that purpose. So, as birds so it is with humans—if you want to fly against the winds, you must also "work" against the prevailing winds.

What is the important lesson of life here: *You cannot determine the direction or the force of the winds. You can only determine the position of your wings to make its force yours. That is how birds fly. That is how you must fly. To say it another way: You work at what you can to make it work for you—not against you.*

This photo below is of a different bird. It was taken from quite a distance, so I missed what the bird was doing beyond my impression of looking a beautiful bird flying across and equally beautiful Florida summer sky; until I came home engaged in my non-scientific research—or perhaps more describe as my ritual of reviewing each photo looking for details—

digitally enhanced like a close up instead of a distant shoot. I was excited to see this bird I photographed flying so high, perhaps to protect its catch—hard at work with its catch carried by its wings and leg and entire body at work—flying high against the wind. But I must note here that birds as in the photo above, birds work at more than flying. It appears they fly in their effort to accomplish their purpose. Flying is not the end of their dreams. It is what get them there. The following is the same bird arriving at its nest to share its catch—wings spread wide.

Nothing is accomplished without work. Nothing is done without action.
Why do birds fly? They work at it.

Birds at Work

I watch a little black bird in my backyard building its nest with patience and purpose—carefully selecting materials from some distance—some hard and soft laid in all the right places. Trip after trip it worked intricately weaving its design into a netted home strong enough to withstand dust-up tropical winds against a tree limb; yet delicate enough to house its tender eggs and young when born. And it never stopped working until it its task was done.

Birds at Work in the Bible:

Genesis 8:8: A dove at Captain Noah's command flew out of the ark to find dry land.

Isaiah 34:15 "The owl nests and lays and hatches her young" to care for them was the theme of her song.

Obediah 1:4 The eagle's nest is set among the stars, so we can see it and say that is who we are.

1 Kings 17:4 Elijah fed by birds: "You will drink from the brook, and I have directed the ravens to supply you with food there"

Psalms 104:12 "The birds of the sky nest by the waters; they sing among the branches"

Reverlation 19:17 "And I saw an angel standing in the sun, who cried in a lowd voice to all the birds flying in midair, Come gather together for the great supper of God."

It is no easy job being a bird.

We live on top of the world—yes!

But it's where we do our best work.

5 "Wonder"

Life from Alternative Perspectives

The fifth "w" is that of "*Wonder.*" When birds fly, they see the world in wonder. From birds taking to the sky is that of appealing to human's spirit to expand their horizons. Like birds in flight that sees the world with expanded vision taking the unlimited advantage that flying above ground offers. It's the "wonder" that birds possess. They can walk or hop around on the ground, yet at a moment's notice take to the open skies. I have often wondered what birds see when they look up? What do they see when they fly high and look down. One thing I am certain—they see the world from a different perspective when they do. They naturally challenge us to do the same— never be afraid to discover different perspectives so prevalent in our world. In a hotel room on the second floor, I walked out early before the sun came up. And at eye level I saw this song bird paused on a wire under a silent moon. It was not singing, perhaps because it was observing as I was the striking detailed image of the moon greeting another tropical day. I know it sounds crazy—but I did wonder what was in that little song bird's mind under what must be to its perspective a very big moon. Nothing in this photo was manipulated in any way like artistic rendering or composition.

Birds use same eyes as on the ground that give them the earth-bound perspective. But then, they have this incredible ability to use their wings and with the same eyes see the same world, but from an entirely different perspective. And they do not fall to the ground when they do. They willingly accept the different perspectives when they do. It is how they are able to navigate on land and in the sky—and some even in the sea. They embrace the different perspective—some needs it to survive and other to thrive. The reality is birds must accept these expanded and dynamic dimensions of earth and sky to fly. Only humans it seems struggle relentlessly to maintain their own limited welled baked perspective—unwilling often to see anything differently from the little piece of land on which they stand. Never from above it. Birds do this all the time. The constantly navigate their world from different perspective. Humans struggle to even look at a simple conversation from the other point of view. Indeed, it is even difficult just to hear it—just to listen for it if it comes from another. Yet the willingness to look at one's self or something from different perspectives is the space where "wonder" is alive, imagination flourishes, and creativity like a bird's egg hatches things that develop wings and fly to the sky.

It is the reason why so much has been lost because the natural "wonder" so active in the early years of life then travel through the dark wilderness of early education that often cripple natural wonderment, and excitement our children have. They are born to fly, and we offer them a walking stick rather than build on their natural "wonder"—their natural desire to see the world in all its shapes, and beauty, from the earth to the sky. It is the difference between being taught an education and experiencing it. In order to fly you must seek—you must develop the "wonder"—the excitement from seeing the world differently.

I had a professor of biology—although he did not much wanted to hear my view on certain aspect of biology because of my conservative theology, I made a consistent effort to listen to his. But he made it easy though, to listen to him. Many things he lectured in glass I forgot. But he did something no other professor after years in college never did. He took the entire class on field trips to specific locations so his students could observe the biological processes he was teaching in the classrooms. We saw it in the field. And an otherwise difficult technical subject of biology became alive in unforgettable ways. He created "wonder" in the perspective of the field study, that was almost impossible to grasp sitting in hard chairs and dry lectures in a class room. It is the way birds navigate, develop, thrive. They constantly looking at their world from different perspective.

Perspective is power. Birds do not take to the sky to escape the earth. They do so to better navigate it—to understand it—to learn how to better live in it—most of all to understand their own critical place in it. When they fly in groups, they each fly with a different perspective of their place, yet despite this they fly together. Something humans work at all their lives and still come up short. It is the "wonder" of nature—the ability and possibility to always grow in wonder of this amazing world—so often obscured by ignorance of nature and our place in it. If only we could learn from the birds to fly in this unlimited space of wonder.

Our astronauts reported how life changing it was to look back and see the earth from above. The difference in the view from above made a difference in their lives below. *Each*

person has more skies in heir mind, heart, spirit and soul than in all the solar systems. It is one of the most unexplored areas of human's existence. Yet, it holds the key to the salvation of the human's race. This is not a cliché. It is the language of nature all around us—humans have the tools to fly and the unique space to use them.

What does it mean to "wonder?" In addition to what I have laid out above it means never to be satisfied or complacent about what you have to achieve—about using your unique "wings" you have been given. It means always being filled with curiosity to learn—especially open to look at something or someone from a different perspective you have maintained. It means to be always open to new ways in which you can use your abilities to advance yourself as well as to help others. For when birds fly they see the wonder of the earth—they do not see themselves when they fly. So, takes a bird eye's view. Look at the wonder all round you and a strange thing will happen.

You will begin to see the wonder inside of you as well. Such wonder is the source of an expanded perspective. It is the wonder of not "keeping up with the Joneses" but looking past them. Wonder is the source of creative thinking because it provides new ways to fly—new ways to reach to the sky. At its most basic level it is the source of personal power to achieve. It is what students in our school must learn as a first principle to develop their natural desire—to wonder.

It means looking at things that amaze you—that give you positive energy. It is like what the Bible said "...*Fix your thoughts on what is true, and honorable, and right, and pure, and lovely, and admirable. Think about these things that are excellent and worthy of praise*" (Philippians 4:8 NLT). The human capacity to fly where eagles fly is given to those who dream; who resist despair with the power of hope; to those who fly in the rain and even in the storm because they know *no storm last forever*. It is the place and space of "wonder" where hope is fuel, dreams are born, victories are won even before and battle begins. To *wonder* is to fly high above all the things that wants to drag you down. **It is to fly where eagles fly when all you have are chicken wings: These are not limitations, just a different gift for different applications in life; that only you are gifted to make. It is that each person has a unique gift. To discover that gift(s) and use it well is what gives real personal power.**

A Butterfly View of "Wonder"

I am not a bird, I am a butterfly—a lower form of existence—perhaps among things that fly. But I am OK with that. For I am yet unique. I have wings that rival any bird in the sky. When you see me moves I know you must wonder where the heck am I going and if I ever would get there with all those twists and sharp turns. You see, I never take a straight path to get any place like all those other birds with wings. But, I always know where I am going and what I need to do to get there. I am equipped with advanced sensors in my body—even in my legs. The information they give me so I can accurately develop my flight plan in "top secret." No one knows as yet how I do it. They are studying me to find out. But its going to take a while, because I use some very advanced and sophisticated aerodynamic maneuvers—calculated through my body related to the unique design of my wings, and the real time winds and changes around me. I do not glide on the wind as other fancy flyers do. I take a different approach—I little butterfly create my own path through the wind. So, sometimes that means some unique moves unlike any other creature that fly. But I know what I am doing flapping my beautiful wings 25 times a second around my fragile little

body. I do the moves with full body maneuvers through the wind—too fast for you to see with your natural eyes. You must slow me down through video technology just to notice what I do. What can you learn from me? Well you have an ongoing stereotype about **beauty and brains** as if they are mutually exclusive. So, to those of you who often confront this. Take a look at me and my friends when we pause for you to get a look. Remember we are small, yet some off the most beautiful creatures that fly—and we fly with the brains to go with it. Do not let your looks determine your life. Do not let your looks determine what you can achieve. Get your sensors out. Establish your flight plan and use all you got to maneuver through the wind of time. If I can control my small fragile body through the wind—even strong ones—heck, you can! That is my lesson to you.

6 "Worry"

Fly to Defend Against Worry

It is revealing of an ancient warrior and King—leader of his people Israel almost three thousand years ago, who as a young man of the field must have seen so many animals around him, traveling the pastures, parries, and hills country of his people. But at a time when he was in severe distress and worry about the circumstances of his life—he selected a bird—a dove to express the solution to his worries. He said "**Oh that I had the wings of a dove! I**

would flee far away and stay in the desert; I would hurry to my place of shelter, far from the tempest and storm" (Psalm 55:6,7 NIV).

I have often reflected on the abundance of birds and wondered where they go in a storm? David concluded where the doves fly was better than where he was. He wanted to have wings to do the same. Birds do not look at the weather report to track a storm to see if it is coming their way as humans needs to do. Indeed, when I was growing up in the Caribbean—before the technology existed to track storms and send real-time information globally—we long notice—information handed down had develop an understanding to listen to the animals that would notify each other and as well as us that a storm is coming. The larger animals bunch up together and seek cover, and the birds disappeared from the sky into their hiding places unknown us. Sometimes, we would see a

late straggler—a bird pouched all along struggling against the wind. But sooner or later it flies away—perhaps having tested the early winds—perhaps to gather information on the strength of the coming storm to let the others know in their hiding places. But, generally when things get tuff birds use their wings—their ability to fly—the gift they have of wings to fly away from the storms. They do not conference about it. They do not send a task force to study it. They do not wait to see it on television as we do. They know a storm is coming they do not waste their time in worry and fret. They use their wings they have been given and fly to safety until the storm passes.

To be successful in life one needs to learn this lesson from the birds: Do not worry over the storms of life for which you have no control. But focus on that which you have control—you do have control over "worrying." The solution to worry is not to worry about your storms— even worst—worrying about worrying. Use the bird's solution—draw on your wings— your abilities, your creativity, your work, your wonder, your will, find your way to act. Take to the sky. There is always a place to go when you employ your wings—like a birds fly you to a safe place away from the storm where you can rest until the storm passes. Birds know that nature never sends a forever storm. Sooner or later the storm passes. And they would take to the sky as if the storm was never there. No storms lasts forever. No fear, no fret. Fly away and find rest. And carry no guilt in that space.

7 "World"

(Detecting your world)

When my daughter was a little mom worked regular hours, and I was her daycare. I took here with me on my construction projects as well as photographic assignments—on high fashion shows and movie set. When she was old enough, I gave her one of my cameras and selectively assisted me on these projects. Especially on construction projects for her safety I had but one rule for her: *Always be aware of what is going on around you.* There could be a nail hiding in a piece of wood—so do not walk on wood—or over debris even when it looks safe. Always walk where you can see the way clear—not just on the ground but especially overhead on ledges— things left overhead that can fall on yours. She is now an adult and never been hurt once. I wished I can say the same about me. As my Dad taught me so I did for her. At an early age I taught her to operate powerful construction equipment like a skid steer—fearless in control and aware what it can do and how to use it—always being aware of what is going on around you. It is a simple practical rule that is very powerful for success. The rule of awareness. For certain animals "awareness" is the only thing that keep them alive. Some animals are assigned that job. In a group they would stand watch, and any sign of trouble they instantly would let the others know; so they all can take cover or other defensive actions. Young elephants are never allowed to travel of the parameters of the herd. They need to first develop awareness of the dangers around them. So they are kept in the safe middle by their older members of the herd until they learn of the dangers around them.

Photo 1. This black hawk pouched on a twig about 150 feet away had no objections. Tall grass and trees gave me cover as I moved closer but was no match for the eyes of this hawk that seems to be able to sense movements in a distance and see behind trees. With the raising of one wing Photo 2 gave me a gentle warning I was close enough. I must have moved too close, or perhaps the rapid shutter sound its disposition certainly changed. I did not notice from a distance; hiding behind the trees moving slowly the change in attitude related to my slow

hidden, I thought movements towards a closer look, until I look at these frames taken in rapid succession. I was not hidden at all from the predator sensibilities of this bird. Its survival, and the survival of other creatures around it depend on awareness—awareness of the surrounding. This predictor bird knows seconds count and calculate within a few it was time to fly. The black-bellied whistling duct allowed me to come much closer still behind trees about 50 feet away was still too close as it went from sitting as I get closer it stood up. Then quickly like the black hawk flew away.

Photo 1 - Sitting

Photo 2 Standing.

Photo 3. Flight away from perceive threat.

8 Wisdom

Beyond Feathers

To get to where you want to go you must take deliberate steps to get there.

Sometimes to get ahead I must share the tree with people different from me.

When you decide to fly it is important to get off to a good start.

Always protect those you love.

Do not be afraid of your path—it's yours. Take it.

Never forget face to face is still the best form of communication.

Even when the mist gathers, like a bird, you can still spread your wings and fly.

You can stand together even when you have different views about it.

Never take the attitude only you alone can fix it. When you need help, ask for it.

Glory not in what you accomplished but that you were privilege to accomplished it.

Genesis 1: 20

And God said, "Let the water teem with living creatures,
and **let birds fly above the earth** in the open expanse of the sky."

With all the creatures God created in the beginning it would appear only birds were created to fly above the earth. But without getting to deep into this. One can conclude God creating birds to fly was to challenge us to do the same. For in time—although it took thousands of years human created instruments and machines to fly miles beyond any bird can go. But the lesson from the bird in regard to wings is more for an earthly application—my point is more down-to-earth. It is that if we are going to fly we need wings like a bird. And God created his crowning creation as human's beings with "wings" to fly. The wisdom from the bird is God gave them wings to fly and so they can. But he also gave humans the ability to fly and to do so with spiritual wings, or "wings of the spirit." This is evident all around us—as "ordinary" people do extraordinary above and beyond even what they thought possible. This is what we aim for here to let each ready know we all have wings, and we are challenge to use them even in the storm.

9 Winning Dreams – Words to be Wise

Epilogue

I have focused on the wisdom of the birds in this book. Perhaps it is because since a boy I have been captivated by the life lessons I have learned from my dad giving me two pigeons. I had no clue in such a short time they would multiply to fifty. I also had no clue how much wisdom I would gain from watching how the grow behave and fly. And I do not think my parents knew how much lessons they were giving me in the small back yard of our home filled with pigeons. They did not know instead of me raising pigeons that they were raising me. This may have started this wonderful journey into lessons from bird land. But it did not end there. From my backyard I have learned there is wisdom in almost everything if you pause to see her there.

So, I have often been fond of that illusive thing call wisdom to see her in everything. All the education in the world is not much without it. Money cannot purchase it, and it is not by race or gene or status that one gains wisdom. She is found in the lives of birds, and the bees. She is even found with big wisdom yet in a small things like an ant—called out for its large store of wisdom action consistently planning so diligently for the future, yet among the smallest of creatures. It is like the

old man in the Bible who by his wisdom delivered a city from destruction yet forgotten even while the citizens shared the fruits of his victory.

Wisdom is difficult to gain quick and easy to ignore. Among the wisest in our land are among and the children in their innocence and truth, and the Old like gold tried in the fire of life are left with such clarity wisdom from the ages. Yet both are among the largest group often ignored on any issue.

God has left us with a rich source of wisdom from everything and most of all from a relationship with Him. He said "if anyone lack wisdom let him ask of God who gives....." (James 1:5). Wisdom is both something to be gained as well as a gift to receive. "Get wisdom, and in all your getting get understanding..." (Proverbs 4:7)

It has been a deliberate life pursuit to seek wisdom in everything. To learn lessons from life and pass on as much as I can to others. One of the difficult issues facing civilization today is the death of wisdom. It appears even the increase of knowledge is suppressing wisdom. The art of reflection, contemplation, and meditation are drifting in the winds of new technologies and statistical analysis, and even AI.

The Wisdom of the Cow

My dad had a job among many others taking care of cows. I participated in chores for the cows as well. I saw them glazing—eating all day long. Yet, when the afternoon came they would get away under a tree for the shade is provides them. And I observe even there their mouths would still be going non-stop. So I wondered why do cows never stop eating. So, I asked my dad what the cows were doing? Why would they chew on nothing? He said, "they are chewing their cod." What was that? They are chewing the food they ate all day long. Then they were just trying to get in. Then they lay down and portion by portion the have a way of bringing it all back up and chew on it again. It is like the importance of meditation. You reflect on what you already heard or experience.

We need to learn the wisdom of the cow. In a busy world we need to learn to fly away. We need to take a pause from the heat of the sun. We need to lie down in green pasters so we can restore our souls. My dad said when the cow lies down and begins to chew it cods, that is the time that it is really eating. All day long it is merely gathering food.

We now live in a world where we gather so much and reflect on so little. Even migrant birds that fly from one time zone to the other know all their rest stops along their way. They never say we'll stop on the next trip. Like clockwork and withing specific time frame they would show up. It is in the wisdom of the cows and the birds each in their own way know the wisdom of the pause. "Come apart and rest awhile" Jesus told his disciples. Notice He said "awhile."

Birds and other creatures that roam the earth among us teach us so much about ourselves. Hope you enjoy this little journey into the world of the wisdom of the birds

Photos of Inspiration and personality

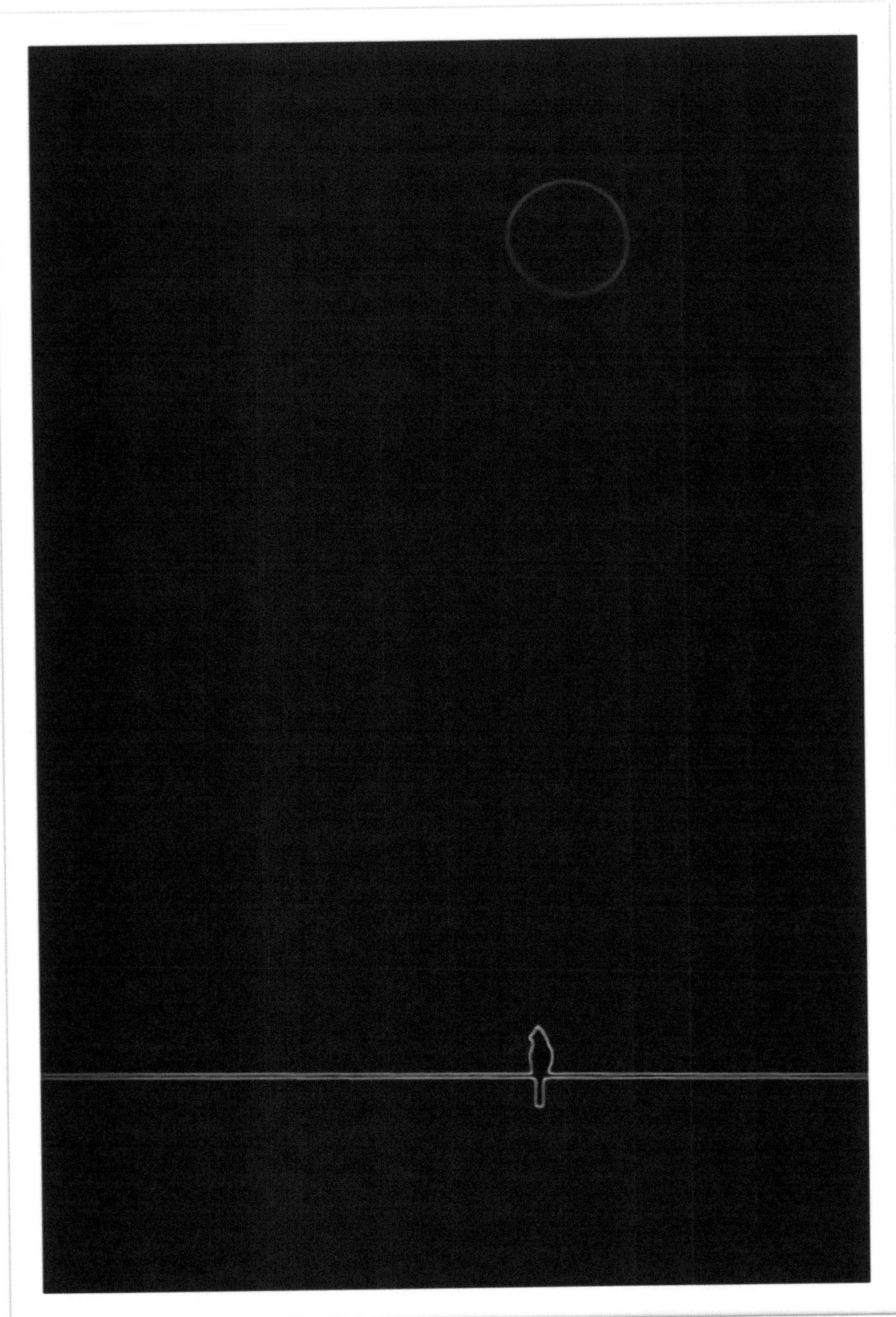

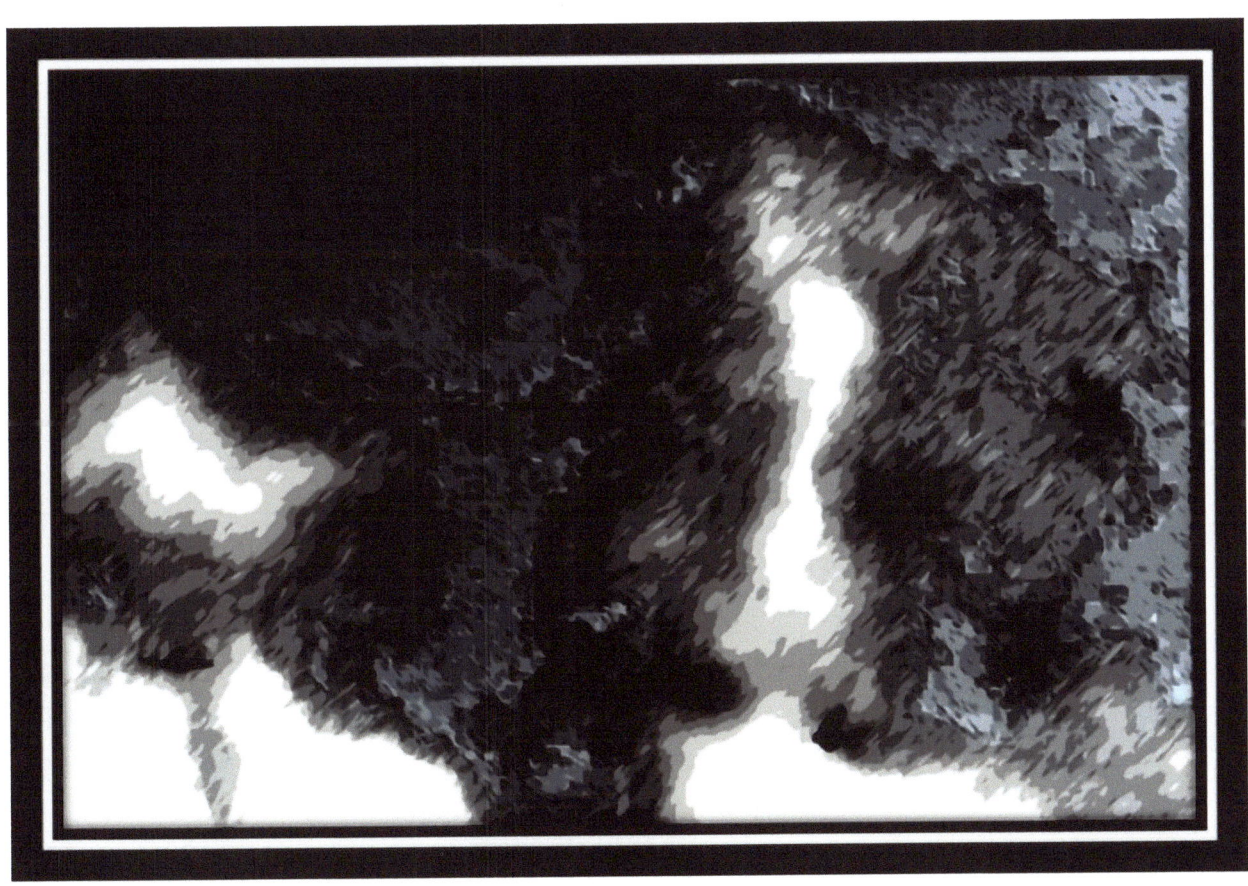

Why Do Birds Fly?

They fly for what the world needs most: Love

In-House Book Review

"A Masterful Blend of Nature's Wisdom and Human Insight. "Dr. Arnold Thompson's "Why Do Birds Fly" is not merely an exploration into avian behavior, but rather an introspective dive into life, wisdom, and the myriad lessons nature offers to humanity. With a narrative that effortlessly weaves through personal memories, biological insights, and spiritual musings, the manuscript offers a captivating blend of science and poetry that is rare in contemporary literature.

From the outset, Thompson delves deep into the habits of birds, drawing nuanced parallels between their survival instincts and our own daily challenges. The writing dances between the analytical and the poetic, with descriptions like the "black-bellied whistling duct" serving as literal observations and metaphors for deeper truths about our nature and the world around us. Yet, what truly sets this work apart is the way in which Dr. Thompson's personal memories, especially the touching anecdotes about his father and their shared experiences with pigeons, anchor the broader lessons from the avian world.

These personal stories add richness and depth to the text, making it both universally relatable and intimately personal. Thompson's musings on wisdom, especially his remarks on how even amidst technological advancements, humanity seems to be drifting away from true wisdom, resonate powerfully. He contrasts the hurried pace of modern life with the contemplative nature of birds, and even cows, urging readers to find their own moments of reflection and understanding.

The book culminates with a powerful statement, drawing from the natural world to pinpoint what our world truly needs – love. This poignant ending ties together the various threads of thought, leaving readers both enlightened and introspective.

In conclusion, "Why Do Birds Fly" is a **gold-standard** manuscript, offering readers not just a fresh perspective on birds but an uplifting and enlightening lens through which to view life itself. It's a text that speaks to the heart and mind, reminding us of the beauty and wisdom inherent in the world around us – if only we take the time to observe and reflect.

—Greg T. of MainSpring Books